PALM BEACH COUNTY
LIBRARY SYSTEM
3650 Summit Boulevard
West Palm Beach, FL 33406-4198

VAMPIRINA
in the
FALL

Written by **Sara Miller**

Illustrated by **Imaginism Studio** and the **Disney Storybook Art Team**

DISNEY PRESS
Los Angeles • New York

First Paperback Edition, June 2018 10 9 8 7 6 5 4 3 2 1
ISBN 978-1-368-01564-6
FAC-029261-18110
Library of Congress Control Number: 2017943601

SUSTAINABLE FORESTRY INITIATIVE
Certified Sourcing
www.sfiprogram.org
SFI-01415

Printed in the United States of America
For more Disney Press fun, visit www.disneybooks.com

Vampirina loves all the seasons.

She loves winter.

She loves spring.

She loves summer.

But of them all, Vee's favorite
season is . . . fall!

In the fall, Vee goes back to school!

Vee's batpack holds her school supplies.

In the fall, the Woodchuck Woodsies go leaf-peeping.

The Woodsies have bake sales, too.
Vee sells her mummy-bear cookies
and flying batcakes.

Vee goes apple picking in the fall.

She makes creepy candy apples, spooky spiced cider, and wormy apple pie!

The weather starts getting colder
in the fall.

It reminds Vee of eerie nights in Transylvania.

And in the fall, Nanpire knits cozy
sweaters for everyone.

Fall is for jumping in piles of crunchy leaves!

Fall is for camping.
And fall is for telling spooky
stories around the campfire.

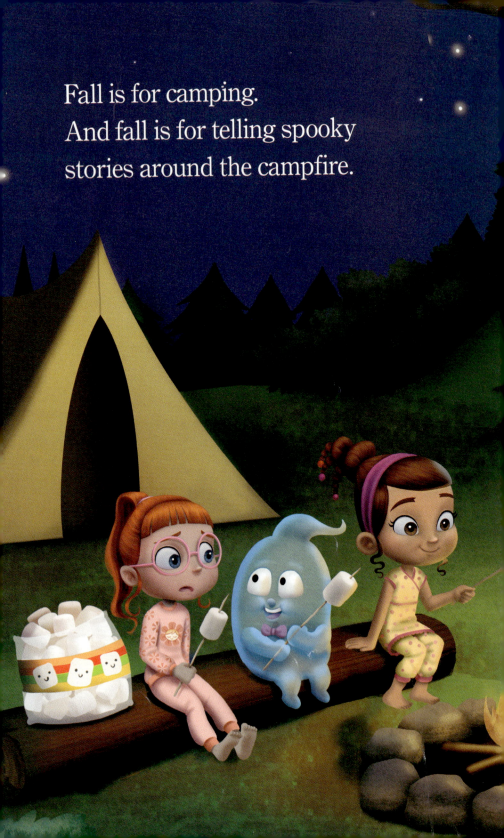

In the fall, Vee goes to the pumpkin patch.

She looks for the best pumpkin to
make a vamp-o'-lantern!

Fall is for Halloween!
Vee's family hangs lots of
cobwebs.

They put spooky cauldrons in every corner.

And they make sure the treat bowls are always full.

Vee's friends dress up in Halloween costumes!
But Vampirina does not need one.
She gets to be herself!

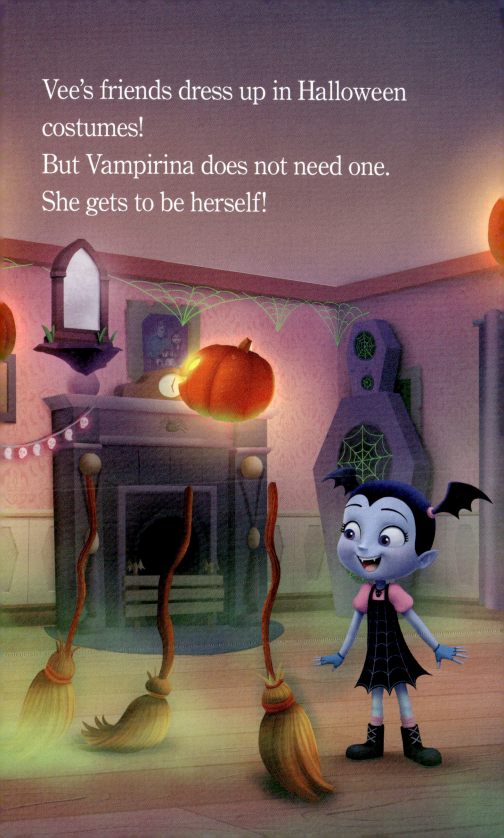

Fall is also for Fangsgiving!
Chef Remy Bones cooks
for days and days.

Vee loves the cobweb stuffing and the monster mashed potatoes.

Her favorite is the pumpkin pie with ghoul whip on top!

But guess what Vee likes most of all.
Being with her family in the fall!